The SpongeBob Movie : Sponge Out Of Water

Storyline

During a fight between the Krusty Krab and Plankton, the secret formula disappears and all of Bikini Bottom goes into a terrible apocalypse. The Bikini Bottomites go crazy and they all believe that Spongebob and Plankton stole the secret formula. The two new teammates create a time machine to get the secret formula before it disappears and also go to some weird places along the way including a time paralex where they meet a time wizard named Bubbles who is a dolphin. The two later get to the time when the formula disappeared and take it back to the present day time. They then realized that it's a fake formula Plankton made when he was taking the real one and the Bikini Bottomites try to destroy Spongebob (Plankton runs away) Spongebob smells Krabby patties and so does everyone else so the Bikini Bottomites follow it (instead of destroying Spongebob) and they arrive at the bank of the surface. Everyone except Spongebob, Patrick, Mr. Krabs, Squidward, Sandy, and a stowaway Plankton go

...

"Booby Traps"?

There you are, my lovely.

What's that?

Take the book?

I don't mind if I do.

At last, it is mine.

Finally, you are mine.

All right. Let's do this. Bare knuckles.

Bring it on, skinny. You don't scare me.

You got any sevens?

Go fish.

Is that all you got?

Man, this is way overdue.

"Once upon a time, under the sea,

"there was a little town
called Bikini Bottom.

"In this town, there was a place
called The Krusty Krab,

"where folks would come to eat a thing
called the Krabby Patty.

"Every greasy spoon has a fry cook,
and the one who worked here

"was named SpongeBob SquarePants."

Who lives in a pineapple under the sea?

SpongeBob SquarePants!

Absorbent and yellow and porous is he

Just hold it. Hold it.

SpongeBob SquarePants!

If nautical nonsense
be something you wish #

SpongeBob SquarePants!

Then drop on the deck
and flop like a fish #

SpongeBob SquarePants!

Stop!

There's only one thing worse
than talking birds, and that would be...

Singing birds!

Okay, I promise not to si-i-i-ng.

Take it from us.

He really does hate singing birds.

Just keep weading.
Pwease, Mr. Piwate, sir.

Come closer while I tell you the tale.

- Okay, start reading.
- No. Not that close!

Yeah.

All right, here we go.

Now, SpongeBob loved his job
as a fry cook

more than anything.

And that is saying a lot

because he loved everything!

He loved his pet snail, Gary.

He loved his best friend, Patrick.

He loved blowing bubbles

and jellyfishing.

He loved making Krabby Patties
for the folks of Bikini Bottom

just as much as they loved eating them.

Why, you may ask,

do they love this
greasy little sandwich so much?

Why did they eat them for breakfast,

lunch,

5

and dinner,

despite their doctor's warnings?

He'll be gone in a week.

Oh, Harold!

It was a secret.

No one was sure what was

in these patties
that made them so delicious.

And, frankly, no one cared,

except for Plankton.

Plankton owned a restaurant
right across the street

from The Krusty Krab,

where no one ate
because the food was really bad.

Now, is that really necessary?

Plankton had made it his life's work
to steal the recipe.

SpongeBob, please,
let's talk about this!

And SpongeBob was
always there to protect it.

But today, things

would be different.

Good morning, SpongeBob!

Morning, Patrick!

You here for
your pre-lunch Krabby Patty?

I'm getting two today.

One for me and one for my friend.

Have I met this friend?

"You know me, SpongeBob."

Enjoy, Patrick's tummy.

Thirteen,

fourteen, fifteen...

Hey, Mr. Krabs, I thought we got
our tartar sauce delivery on Thursday.

Tartar...

Sauce?

Bull's-eye!

Plankton!

So it's a food fight he wants, eh?

Welcome to Air Plankton.

Please put your seat backs
and tray tables up

as we're now approaching
our final destination.

Okay, Patrick, load the potatoes!

Mashed or scalloped, sir?

No, Patrick. Raw.

Sir, yes, sir!

Locked and loaded!

Don't worry, little formuler,
you'll be safe in this

safe.

Fire!

Potatoes?

He's closing in!

I think we have a few minutes
before he gets here.

He's right on top of us!

Hey, it's raining fries!

It's gonna take a lot more than
potatoes to bring this baby down.

Or maybe not.

Wait a minute, Patrick, look!
He's got a tank!

Well, Krabs, you're certainly
in a pickle now!

Hey, it's raining pickles!

Now it's raining...

Tanks.

You're welcome!

Finland.

Your orders, sir!

I'll have two
Krabby Patties-extra ketchup,

extra mustard, and hold the mayo.

Wrong channel!

Your orders, sir!

Extra ketchup! Extra mustard!
Hold the mayo!

Yes, sir!

Extra ketchup! Extra mustard!

Hold the mayo!

Unleash the condiments!

With relish.

Excuse me.

Hello?

Hello?

- Guess y'all don't want my money.
- Money?

Thank you! Come again!

I can't hold the mayo any longer!

Mayo? Well, it's going to
take a lot more than mayo to stop...

Now what?

I just remembered,
I don't work for Mr. Krabs!

Robot! Robot!

Robot! Giant robot!

Robot! Robot!

Mr. Krabs, Plankton's here
and he's got a giant robot!

Quick, boy, bar the door!

Got it!

I'll take one secret formula

to go.

Oh, barnacles. I'm out of gas?

I'm not through yet.

I've got something that will make
you hand over that formula.

Something you can't resist.

Money!

Yes!

That's... That's... That's impossible!

Well, it was full of money
just last week.

And then I bought that airplane
and built that tank.

Sounds to me like
someone's just a wee bit broke!

Well, Krabs, I guess you've won.

I've spent every penny I've ever made
trying to put you out of business.

Except this one. My last penny.

Besides, what can I do
with one measly cent anyway?

You could give it to me.
Just a suggestion.

Here, take it.

You've taken everything else. Why not?

Well, Plankton,
like a reheated Krabby Patty,

you've been foiled again.

I guess this means the secret formula
is safe forever, right, Mr. Krabs?

It sure does, boy.

Why don't you scurry along?

Thanks for coming! Have a nice day!

He's been out there
crying for 20 minutes.

Pathetic.

I'm just going to
go out there and gloat a little.

Cyclops to Laptop. Come in, Laptop.

"Laptop." You do realize
that nickname is demeaning?

I have twice
the processing power of a laptop.

Never mind. Maintain radio silence.

Finally!

A pressure plate, eh, Krabs?

Amateur hour.

Perfect!

Not a bad likeness.

Good enough to fool that idiot Krabs.

Easy, easy.

Plankton's broke!

Look at Mr. Krabs go.

I've never seen him
gloat this hard before.

Hey, well, Plankton,

me bunions are telling me
it's time to stop gloating.

Looks like you're
falling apart at the seams.

Poor me.

- Sob, sob.
- A robot?

Plankton?

That ain't good.

Initiating lockdown sequence.

Me formuler!

No, no, no! No!

Squidward! Open up!

Victory dance. Boo-ya.

Give me that!

Come on, SpongeBob, join me!

And we'll be rich and powerful,
until I eventually betray you.

- Join me!
- No! Never!

I'm on Team Krabs for life!

Plankton!

What? Where'd it go?

Wait a minute. Molecular deconstruction?

I proved that to be
a scientific impossibility seven times!

Wait a minute.

I think I forgot to empty
Gary's litter box today.

Where's me formuler, Plankton?

I... I don't know! It just disappeared!

Why should I believe you,
you lying liar?

Normally, I'd agree with you, Mr. Krabs,

but this time he's telling the truth.
It just vanished!

It's true!

Mr. Krabs, I'm telling you
he's innocent!

What are you going to do, Krabs?

Pour hot oil on me?

Or put bamboo shoots under my nails?

No. Knock, knock.

Knock-knock jokes?
I can do this all day, Krabs.

Knock, knock.

Oh, boy. Who's there?

Jimmy.

Jimmy who?

Jimmy back my formuler, Plankton!

Well, that's stupid,
but how is it torture?

You'll see.

"Jimmy back my formula"?

I get it!

Make it stop, Krabs! Make it stop!

Mr. Krabs? SpongeBob, zip it!

Thank you, Squidward.

The customers are getting restless!

They're asking for refunds.

Refunds.

Refunds?

Refund! Refund!

Listen up, boy. Get in there

and make me customers
some Krabby Patties!

All right, Plankton...

SpongeBob! What's wrong, boy?

We're out of Krabby Patties?

How can we make more Krabby Patties
without the secret formula?

You've got to have
that formuler memorized by now!

But as you are aware, sir,

the employee handbook clearly states,
and I quote,

"No employee may, in part or in whole,

"commit the Krabby Patty secret formula
to any recorded written or visual form,

"including memories, dreams,
and/or needlepoint."

Curse you, fine print!

Refund! Refund! Refund!

Stop!

I'm not your enemy!

Plankton is your enemy!

So is he an anemone or a plankton?

Well, someone had to do it.

But Mr. Krabs...

He took this from you!

- Krabby Patty...
- I can almost taste it.

Mr. Krabs, Plankton didn't take
the secret formula.

Not now, SpongeBob!

Hey! I ordered a double Krabby Patty!

So join me! Help get the formuler back,

and I'll give each and every one of
you a free Krabby Patty!

No! Wait!

Even better, a slight discount!

To The Chum Bucket!

But he didn't do it.

I had it right in my greedy little mitts,
and then... Poof!

And now it's gone. Gone forever.

I was so close to
gaining the people's respect-slash-fear.

Plankton?

When will my
frustration-slash-humiliation end?

- Plankton?
- Not now, hon!

I'm ranting-slash-raving.

All right, what is it?

Well, I was trying to tell you
there's an angry mob outside.

But now they're inside.

I just work here.

We'd like to have a word with you!

You all look very hungry.

Can I get anybody a Chum Burger?

Enough with the niceties, Plankton!

This is the last time
I'm going to ask you.

Where is me formuler?

I told you, Krabs, I don't have it.

Wrong answer.

Stop!

All right, Mr. Krabs,
let me get in on this.

What's going on around here?

You may want to
step back a little, Mr. Krabs.

This could get messy.

Let's hope so.

So you won't talk, eh, Plankton?

I didn't want to have to do this.

Plankton, here comes the pain.

Soap in the eye, eh? Diabolical!

No! Stop! Don't!

Wait. That didn't look painful.

Mr. Krabs, you may not understand
what I'm about to do today,

but someday we'll look back
and have a good laugh.

Wait a minute.

Hey, they're getting away!

Sorry, Mr. Krabs!

So, you've been running
a long con on me, eh?

All these years you've been
working for Plankton!

They're in cahoots!

Yeah, I guess
that's a short way of saying it.

Stop that bubble!

Please tell me
there's something soft below me.

- Nope.
- Nope.

SpongeBob!

You were like an underpaid son to me.

I would've expected Squidward
to stab me in the back.

What?

But SpongeBob?

Me most trusted employee?
Working with me sworn enemy?

You know what this means, Mr. Squidward.

We get the rest of the day off?

No!

This be but a harbinger
of what I fear lies ahead.

For you. For me.

For all of Bikini Bottom!

The Krabby Patty
is what ties us all together!

Without it, there will be
a complete breakdown of social order.

A war of all against all!

Dark times are ahead.

Dark times indeed!

Seriously?

Aren't you overreacting a bit?

Welcome to the apocalypse,
Mr. Squidward.

I hope you like leather.

I prefer suede.

And so Bikini Bottom became

an apocalyptic cesspool forevermore.

The end.

Wait a minute. That's a terrible ending.

- This is bad. Really bad.
- What? What?

SpongeBob's in trouble
and the story's over?

Ouch. Ouch. Ouch.

Hey, call a therapist!

I have anxiety!

There is no way that
that's the end of this story.

Of course it is. I'll show you.

Just turn around.

All right.

Hey!

I need that to fly, you jerk.

"The

"End"!

That's not the end!

Of course it is!

- Unhand that book!
- You let go of that!

Let go, you numbskull!

You better keep reading, Mr. Pirate,

or else!

I know I shouldn't be littering,
but that ending was rubbish!

Rubbish!

Good morning, Squidward.
I'll have the usual.

With cheese.

We're out of Krabby Patties right now!

No Krabby Patties?

No!

Look what's become of Bikini Bottom.

We've really gotta get
that formula back.

Get the secret formula, you say?

Excuse me, I need a moment.

With that formula,
I could rule the world!

You know I can hear you, right?

Well, what do we do now?

Now we work together.
You know, teamwork.

What's "tee-am work"?

No, Plankton, teamwork.

Tee-am work.

- Teamwork.
- Tie-'em work.

- Teamwork.
- Tie 'em up!

- Say "team," like a sports...
- Team.

- Team. Now say "work."
- Work.

Put them together. What do you got?

Time bomb work.

Getting better!

Now, Bikini Bottom Action News!

Hey, Patrick!

Krabby Patty, Krabby Patty,
Krabby Patty, Krabby Patty!

Krabby Patty, Krabby Patty, Krabby...

Krabby Patty, Krabby...

Krabby Patty...

Krabby...

Krabby!

Come on, tummy,
it's gonna be a long day.

We interrupt your regular program
for an important news bulletin.

Perch Perkins reporting live
from downtown Bikini Bottom.

Complete chaos here today
as our town attempts to deal with

a sudden and complete shortage
of Krabby Patties.

Events here have
this reporter wondering,

what is the secret ingredient
in Krabby Patties anyway?

It's love!
The secret ingredient is love!

No more Krabby Patties?

If I'd have known that,
I'd have chewed it slower.

What the corndog is that?

Come on, Plankton, it's easy!

It means, I help you, you help me,
and when we accomplish our goal,

then we do hands in the middle.

Hands in the middle?
No, no. Sounds idiotic.

Besides, the two of us
are no match for that cranky mob!

We could probably
use a few more tee-am works.

That's exactly what I was thinking!

Wait, what are you doing?

I need Krabby Patties!

Patrick, what are you doing?

Krabby Patties!

Vandalizing stuff.

Isn't that your house?

Hey, what's with all the questions?

Who are you guys?

It's me, your best friend! SpongeBob?

Yeah?

Well, if you're SpongeBob,
then what's the secret password?

Uh...

Correct! It is you!

SpongeBob!

- SpongeBob.
- Patrick!

SpongeBob!

Why aren't you at The Krusty Krab
making Krabby Patties?

Well, I'd love to,
but the formula's gone.

Yeah, Mr. Krabs says
you and Plankton took it.

No, that's not what happened.

It just disappeared.

We're putting a team together
to find it.

A team?

Pick me! Pick me! Pick me!

Okay, Patrick, you're in.

I don't know, SpongeBob.

What exactly does this clown
bring to the tee-am?

He brings loyalty, Plankton.

Loyalty. Isn't that right, Patrick?

Yeah, yeah, loyalty.

I've got SpongeBob!

He's over here!

Let's go get him!

Come on, SpongeBob,
let's get out of here!

Patrick!

Patrick, why are you doing this?

Because I need

Krabby Patties!

Hurry up! I'm hungry!

Over here!

Guys, am I still on the team?

Hey, what are you looking at?

Sandy!

Sandy!

Sandy?

Sandy, are you home?

Gee, Plankton, I wonder where she is.

What is all this stuff?

Sandy?

Don't touch that!

Incoherent muttering.

Sandy? Are you okay?

Okay?

Have you looked outside?
Does that seem "okay" to you?

I'm trying to figure out
what happened to society.

If we don't fix it soon,
there won't be anything left to fix!

Sandy?

The lack of Krabby Patties
has driven her mad.

And I think I figgered it out.

Look.

When this came down from above,

29

I knew it could only mean one thing.

And that would be?

It means it's the end!

The sandwich gods are angry with us!

- Sandwich gods?
- Sandwich gods?

I just don't know
how we're going to appease them!

You got any other friends
who aren't dim bulbs or nut jobs?

Well, I have one friend
who's loyal to the very end.

Gary, I'm home.

Gare-bear?

Gary?

Gary?

Revolting!

But it means Gary is close by!

Gary, I'm back!

Hey, Gary, Plankton and I need you
to help us find the Krabby Patty formula

and fix Bikini Bottom.

What do you mean,
you don't have to do as I say anymore?

What do you mean, "King of Snails"?

Gary The Snail, you get down here
right now and join this team!

What do you mean, "Seize them"?

Why are you running?

Because they're right on our tail.

Right, snails.

Well, so much for your tee-am.

Putting together a team is a lot harder
than I thought it would be!

This way!

We better get out of here
until things cool off.

Everything we know and love
has been destroyed.

Yeah, looks like they're gonna have to

change the name of Bikini Bottom
to Dirty Bottom.

Right, SpongeBob?

That's kind of gross, Plankton.

Yeah. Yeah, too soon, huh?

This feels like it really is "the end".

Don't worry, SpongeBob,

we'll find the secret formula

and everything will go back
to the way it was,

you know, all happy and junk.

Now let's try and get some sleep.

Yeah, I guess you're right.

Here you are. Feel comfy?

You know, Plankton,

I think you might know a little bit more
about teamwork than you let on.

Good night, SpongeBob.

Good night, Plankton.

"Good night," indeed.

That's right, SpongeBob, sleep.

You're hiding that formula
in there somewhere.

Well, here goes nothing.

What is this place?

Fudge fight!

It's all over me!

It's so sweet in here!

I think my eyeball
is getting a toothache!

Hello, Plankton.

Come and play with us.

Hurry

before we melt.

So much sweetness.

I think I'm going to be sick!

Daddy!

Plankton? Plankton!

I just had the craziest dream!
And you were in it!

I'm sure it was nothing.

Now go back to sleep.

Were you in my brain?

What? No! That's crazy talk!

Then why is there
cotton candy on your antenna?

Because, because...

Okay, fine, I was in your brain.

What were you doing in there?

What do you think I was doing?

Looking for the secret formula.

- What?
- Don't act so innocent.

You knew what I was up to.

That's why you're pretending
not to know the formula.

I'm not pretending!

I can't believe you thought I was lying.

Hey, don't take it personally.

I just assume everyone is lying.

That is a horrible way

- to live your life.
- Whatever.

It is! And if we're going
to be on the same team...

Maybe I don't want to be on the tee-am!
You think of that?

But, Plankton, everything's better
when you're part of a team.

You're not going
to start singing, are you?

- # Teamwork! #
- Oh, brother.

We can do anything when we have teamwork

Don't you think so, my friend?

No, tee-am work

Is getting in the way
of my schee-am work #

What don't you comprehend?

But working together is the key

Nothing's impossible
when it's you and me #

I'm doing just fine on my own

Work is no fun when you do it alone

If I want it done right,
I'll do it by myself #

But what if you need
something on a higher shelf? #

But I'm the target Of a very scary,
crazy post-apocalyptic mob!#

Well, that's exactly
why you need a partner #

Helping you with this important job

I'll be the hammer, you'll be the nail

I'll be the boat and you'll be the sail

I'm the flower, you're the aroma

Right now I wish I was in a coma

Come on.

I'm here for you and you're here for me

It's better when you plus me equals we

Working together in harmony

Side by side, we can reach our dreams

'Cause nothing's impossible

When we're a team!

All right, you can put me down.

Well...

That's one minute of my life
I'll never get back.

Not without a time machine.

Wait a minute. Hold that thought.

Now back up.

Slow down.

Not without a time machine.

Yes!

- SpongeBob, you're a genius!
- I am?

If we build a time machine,

we can go back to before
the formula disappeared.

Before society broke down.
Before we became the hunted!

That sounds great, Plankton,
but how do we build a time machine?

Well, first we'll need
a computer powerful enough

to calculate the intricacies
of time travel.

Where would we get one of those?

There she is. My computer wife.

They've got her tied up
in the back room.

I've never seen
this many people at The Chum Bucket.

I've never seen anyone there.

Now was that really necessary?

Cause the food's really bad.

Come on! Really?

How are we gonna
sneak past those guards?

Well, what do we have here?

We better hurry.
Those guys really hate tires.

We'll never get in. The door's locked.

Wait. The window is open.

Come on, Plankton,

it's time for some teamwork.
Give me a boost.

Okay. Wait a minute, no!

Just a little higher, Plankton.

Plankton?

Why don't you boost me up instead?

Yeah, good thinking.

Come on, SpongeBob, come on!

We're in!

There's a guard over there.

Let's take the key from around his neck.

We're gonna have to be very quiet.

Let's walk on the tips of our toes.

Will you stop playing that tiny piano?

You're gonna get us caught.

Sorry.

Now just reach over and grab it.

Halt! Who goes there?

Stop! Pull it over his head!

Stop, stop, stop!

Let me get up there.

Help me.

What?

No!

Plankton, help!

I'll rock him,
you tell him a bedtime story.

Once upon a time

there was a big fat pink idiot
who went to sleep. The end!

Nice try, but it's
gonna take more than that to...

I told you, I don't have the formula,

you monsters!

- Hey, baby, how are you?
- Plankton!

My hero! You must need something,

otherwise you wouldn't have come back.

Plankton has a plan
to save Bikini Bottom.

It doesn't matter, Plankton.
Krabs knows all your plans.

He's been through my hard drive
looking for the secret formula.

I never had it.
But we're going to get it.

We're gonna go back in time to steal
the formula before it disappeared.

Time travel!

Where are you gonna find
a computer that can do that?

Wait a minute!

I've never carried a head before.

You'll get used to it.

It's still warm.

So you won't talk, huh?

Let some air out of him.

Is this where
we're gonna build our time machine?

Sure. It's got everything we need.

A photo booth.

A cuckoo clock.

Some day-old chips.

Now all we have to do is build it.

- Oh, no, you don't!
- Hey, my pitch pipe!

I need it. For the time machine.

Okay.

Installed!

I did it!

No, we did it!

Wait. We did do it.

As a tee-am.

- A team.
- Whatever.

Working together in harmony

Side by side, we can reach our dreams

'Cause nothing's impossible
When we're a team #

Okay, now for the brains!

Okay, Plankton, this is it.

It's gonna take all my processors
and energy to power this time machine.

So if you have anything
you wanna tell me,

you better tell me now.

Well, Karen...

I know I've taken you for granted
all these years, and...

...I, I just wanted to say,

I'm glad you're on my tee-am.

Oh, Sheldon, that's the sweetest thing
you've ever...

Plankton, are you crying?

No, no, no!

It's just one of the hazards
of having a giant eyeball.

There's always stuff getting in there.

Anyway, where were we?

Say "cheese."

Cheese!

According to my calculations,

The Krusty Krab should be right here!

What's that over there?

- SpongeBob?
- Patrick?

Is it really you?

- Yes, Patrick, it's...
- Finally!

The Great Krabby Patty Famine is over!

Great Krabby Patty Famine?
What year is this?

It's Thursday.

According to my calculations,

we've only gone
four days into the future.

Where is everybody?

They all gave up on you. But not me!

Cause I'm not very smart.

Where is The Krusty Krab?

Right where it's always been!

I think we may be
lost in time, Plankton.

Maybe we should ask
this guy for directions.

Excuse me, sir?
Can you tell us when we are?

Who dares disturb
The One Who Watches?

The One Who Watches?

Your name is The One Who Watches?

No, my true name is

Bubbles.

Bubbles?

What kind of a name is Bubbles?

It is my ancient dolphin name.

So what's a dolphin doing out here
in the middle of space?

My kind have been
watching and protecting

the galaxy for...

10,000 years!

So you're the one
keeping the meteors from hitting us.

Yes, I am.

And I could really do
with a potty break.

Would you mind keeping an eye on things?

Sure thing.
But what am I keeping my eye on?

What are you doing?

I'm watching.

We don't even know
what we're watching for.

Maybe we should split up the workload.

You watch the one with the big red eye,

I'll watch the one
with the ringy thingies.

Like a team.

Okay, mine's moving.

Mine, too.

No, this doesn't seem right.

Should we call Bubbles?

Let's give him a minute.
He's been holding it for 10,000 years.

I'm pretty sure
that wasn't supposed to happen.

Come on, Plankton,
we got to clean this up

before Bubbles gets back!

Much better. Yes.

You two are free to go.

What happened to Saturn and Jupiter?

You were supposed to...

Keep them from smashing into each other!

Sorry.

Now I am going to lose my job!

And you will lose your lives.

Quarter me!

Plankton?

SpongeBob!

Plankton?

SpongeBob?

Who are you two supposed to be?

I'm you, from the future.

And I'm him from the future.

So you traveled back through time

to help me? Great thinking.

Nope. He's helping me.

But he's the enemy!

Was the enemy. Now we're a team.

What? A tee-am?

A team!

All right, go get the formula.

What have I become?

All right, Plankton.

Do you have
flying boatmobiles in the future?

We only came back
from the day after tomorrow, dimwit.

Are there rocket packs?

- Did they outlaw clothes in the future?
- No!

Then why are you naked?

Because they don't make
clothes in my size.

Hold still, you!

If you're from the future,
what am I gonna say next?

- Something moronic?
- Wow.

Hey, hurry up over there!

That ain't good.

Initiating lockdown sequence.

Come on, SpongeBob,
we gotta get out of here!

- Got it!
- Come on!

That was crazy!

So that's what teamwork is.

All those years I tried
to make you mine,

and I finally did it.

I mean, we did it!

And so it would seem that

our heroes have accomplished
all they had set out to do.

Now that's an ending.

Andy, cue the music.

Oh, no.

That's not the end.

So you mean the ending
might be even happier?

Here we go!

Land ho!

Mom, where's my towel?

What?

- Dude, look at that.
- What?

I'm coming! Come on, you lazy people!

Out of my way! I'm coming!

Out of there!

Sorry!

- Too fast!
- Slow down!

- I'm coming!
- No, no!

Yeah!

All right, you feathered rats,
time to shove off!

What? Why?

Well, I can't have you pooping
all over my restaurant, can I?

Restaurant? I thought

this was a pirate ship.

It is.

But it is also...

My very own food truck!

A what?

You know, a restaurant on wheels.

- Like a garbage truck.
- No!

Are you trying to
scare away my customers?

Well, we're not leaving
till we see how the story ends.

No problem.

You guys like
a little snack while you wait?

- Sure, I'll take a curdled milk.
- How about a fish head?

And a French fry covered in sand.

Who wants some...

hot wings?

Wait a minute. Where's Kyle?

Which one of you is next?

He's a madman!

Let's get out of here!

You crazy, man! You crazy!

Bye-bye, Mr. Poop.

Now I can get my gold sticker.

Hey, Mr. Piwate.

I wouldn't go in there if I were you.

I can't fly without my feathers.

Where to, Mac?

Just dwive.

Squidward!

Still out of Krabby Patties.

Does anyone have a picture of ketchup?

I done figgered it out!

We have angered the sandwich gods
and only a sacrifice will appease them!

Well, that sounds reasonable.

Soon our post-apoca-whatchamacallit
will be over,

and Krabby Patties
will rain down from above!

Rain down? Well, that's no good.

How will I get me money?

You don't like that idea?
Then we'll sacrifice you!

Sacrifice! Sacrifice!

It's not a good idea to have a sacrifice

on an empty stomach.

Who wants a Krabby Patty?

SpongeBob, is that me formuler?

Oh, happy day!

I missed you so much.

Where was it? Where did you find it?

Well, Plankton and I
built a time machine

out of an old photo booth
and then we added...

- Cheese!
- Patrick, wait!

It's okay, everyone.

The post-apocalypse is almost over!

Ain't that right, SpongeBob?

"Eugene, eat my

"subaquatic air bubbles.
Love, Plankton"?

You grabbed the wrong bottle!

I'm sorry, Mr. Krabs!

That's okay, SpongeBob.

We'll just have to sacrifice
the two of you then.

Prepare them for the sacrifice!

I bring a message from the dawn of time!

What is it, Patrick?

Run!

Squidosaurus rex!

Well, Plankton,

I guess we failed
to accomplish our goals.

"We"?

But even failure hurts a little less
when you do it as a team, right?

This is all your fault!

My fault?

You're the one who stole
the wrong secret formula.

I didn't know there were two bottles.

Of course you didn't!

Because you got cotton candy for brains!

No, seriously, he really does.

Well, we wouldn't even be in this mess
in the first place,

if you weren't so selfish and evil.

I was selfish and evil,

until you ruined everything
with your "teamwork"!

You take that back!

You are the worst teammate ever!

No!

Oh, my Neptune, he's mixing
garbage and recycling!

Look at me.

Why, I've become like all of you.

Savage.

Fear-ridden.

Selfish.

An entire town of formerly good citizens

turned into heartless freaks,

bent on their own self-prever...

Self-preter...

- "Preservation?"
- Yes!

We've become alienated from each other.

Each one an island unto himself,

concerned only with ourselves.

And in the name of all fishhood,

I am not about to let that happen!

And so,

if a sacrifice is needed to restore
Bikini Bottom to its former glory...

Then I am willing
to take one for the team!

You heard him!

Sacrifice!

Sacrifice! Sacrifice!

Sacrifice!

Sacrifice! Sacrifice!

Let the sacrifice begin!

Patties! Patties!

And I thought my friends were primitive.

Don't cry, me boy.

Everything's going to be fine, for us.

I'm not crying, Mr. Krabs.

I smell Krabby Patties!

That's right.
Keep thinking happy thoughts.

Now!

Sacrifice! Sacrifice!

The boy's right.

My leg!

I smell 'em, too!

Okay, SpongeBob, go get it!

Wait. You mean we can
just take this stuff off?

Go find that Krabby Patty!

Come on, everybody!

I've got some Krabby Patty
orders to fill!

It's coming from over there!

Come on, guys,
I think it's just over this hill.

How do you expect us
to go up to the surface?

We won't be able to breathe!

All right, all secondary characters
come with me.

- Yeah, I'm with you guys.
- No way, Squidward.

You're going up there with us.

My feet hurt.

Patrick, you don't have feet.

It's not fair! You have feet.

Sandy has feet. Squidward has feet.

Actually, I have four feet.

It's not about feet.

What is it about, then?

It's about being a team
and sticking together, no matter what!

The only way
we're going up there is if some

fairy godmother shows up
and helps us breathe air.

- Bubbles!
- SpongeBob, you know this guy?

Don't hurt us!
We're sorry we got you fired.

Hurt you?

Why, I traveled back
through time to thank you.

I've been stuck in that job for eons.

I needed a change,

but I was too afraid to go for it.

Well, Bubbles, I'm glad we could help.

Now it is my turn to help.

I can get you safely to the surface.

Now!

Quick, all of you, get in my mouth.

Come on, guys, let's go!

There's no way I'm climbing
into some dolphin's mouth.

Yeah. This guy just wants a free lunch.

Guys, if Bubbles has the courage
to quit his dead-end, nowhere job

and travel back through time to help us,

then we need to have the courage to...

Well, I never thought
I'd be eaten by a dolphin.

No, if he was eating us,

he'd be chewing us up
and we'd be going down there.

This is what you call riding in style.

Not a lot of legroom in here.

Well, maybe if you didn't
have four feet!

Note to self:
Never stow away in a gym sock.

What's happening? I feel tingly!

My neck!

I've done all I can.

The rest is up to you.

Thank you, Bubbles!

Farewell, SpongeBob.

Farewell, Bubbles.

Now to update my...

Resume!

Fresh air! How I've missed you.

This place smells awful!

Come on, guys.

Let's get the Krabby Patty formula
and save Bikini Bottom.

What is this place?

I have a bad feeling about this.

Maybe this guy knows where we are.
He looks smart.

He's got five heads.

Sir? Could you tell us
where to find a Krabby Patty?

Hey, my friend's talking to you!

What?

A giant, hairy porpoise!

It's beached!

It's suffering. Poor thing.

Y'all, those aren't porpoises.

- All hands on deck!
- Oh, brother.

We need to get these guys
back in the water.

Come on! Push!

- Heave!
- Ho!

- Heave!
- Ho!

Put your back into it!

Come on, push!

Well, I guess this is where that
horrible smell was coming from.

Excuse me, do you know where we can get
a Krabby Patty around here?

Invaders!

You get out of my sister's sand castle!

Mom!

Where have you been all my life?

Oh, Frank.

That feels so good.

Gross!

Oh, hey, Squidward.

Sandy!

The Krabby Patty!

I think I see where it's coming from!

SpongeBob, you will not believe the size
of the ice creams here.

I wonder what
other giant snacks they have.

Cotton candy?

If you ate all that,
you'd have enough energy

to run around the whole world!

When is the sugar gonna wear off?

Hey, guys, I smell Krabby Patties!

I think it's this way!

Don't leave me, Squidward!

- Now what?
- We're never going to make it!

- Heave!
- Ho!

We're doing it, guys!

Dude, watch out!

Hold on!

SpongeBob!

- Lean!
- Starboard!

- What the...
- What?

"Home of the Krabby Patty"?

But The Krusty Krab
is the home of the Krabby Patty!

Mr. Krabs, what are we gonna do?

$8.99 for a Krabby Patty?

Why didn't I think of that?

You!

Cease and desist
that unauthorized patty flipping!

Yeah, that's my job!

How did you get here?

You cannot breathe air.

Well, there was this magical dolphin

from the future who shot us
out of his blowhole, and...

Wait! Wait.

That's not in the book.

Book?

There is no magical dolphin
in this story.

What story?

The story of how Bikini Bottom
was brought to its knees

when its beloved Krabby Patty formula

was stolen by me,

Burger Beard.

How does it end?

Well, let me see.

It looks like

Burger Beard becomes the richest

food truck proprietor in all the land.

But how did you steal the formula?

That was easy.

I simply rewrote the story, and...

Poof!

Me formuler!

What do you mean, rewrote the story?

Watch this.

"The brave

"and handsome

"Burger Beard

"banished our poor heroes

"to be stranded on

"Pelican Island!"

"The End"!

This looks bad.

And these guys look hungry!

Look out!

Nice. So this is what teamwork gets you.

Here! Take Squidward, you vile beasts!

I want to be on a new team.
This one's broken.

Sandy, you're smart. You have any ideas?

I ain't been too smart
since I found this old piece of paper!

- What?
- Incoming!

Wait a minute!

Now all we need is some ink!

Which Squidward has helpfully provided.

It happens when I'm nervous.

Whatever you're going to do,
make it quick!

They're closing in on us!

I'm gonna write us an ending.

Will it be a happy ending?

It's going to be superpowered!

I'll show you a happy ending.

Patrick!

Hey, I got feet!

What is in these things?

We'll take one secret formula to go!

Clear the area, citizens.

There's going to be
some serious aft-kicking here.

But I banished you.

Sour Note?

My tiny little eardrums!

Hey, hey, wait! Hold on! Hold on!

Wait! Wait! Customers!

Wait, please!

Mr. Superawesomeness,

take him down.

Maybe we should have picked
a better superpower for you, Patrick.

Let's see you get out of this one!

Get ready for the Invinci-Bubble!

No!

My book!

All right, team,
time for hands in the middle!

Yes!

Oh, yeah.

Great job, guys. We did it!

What?

Sandy? Is that you?

You can call me The Rodent!

Hey, where'd the pirate go?

It looks like Burger Beard forgot
the first rule of mobile fry cooking.

Always batten down your grease traps.

Follow that grease, team!

There she blows.

Oh, no, you don't.

He's after the book!

Sandy, use your squirrel powers!

Roger that!

She's never gonna make it!

Everyone...

Lean!

That's what you get.

Come here.

The book!

Sour Note!

All right, Burger Beard,
prepare to be teamworked!

I'm going to scrub my armpits with you.

I don't get it.

Because you're a sponge.

Duh.

Get him, The Rodent!

Consider him roasted!

Aw, nuts! I'm all out of nuts!

Justice is best soft served.

Patrick, I should have
never doubted your powers!

I can't think of a sweeter way to go.

It's all mine!

Not so fast, Booger Beard!

Me formuler.

This will make you feel a little butter.

Not melted butter!

Mr. Krabs!

Oh, yeah!

They're beautiful!

Patrick!

I gotcha!

SpongeBob!

- Patrick?
- Talk to me, buddy.

I'm... I'm seeing a bright light.

Is this better?

Much. Thank you.

But the discomfort I feel
in my eyes is nothing

compared to the shame I feel
for letting down the Patty.

For letting down Bikini Bottom.

Yeah, SpongeBob, you really blew it.

No, Patrick, we blew it, as a team.

Nope. This one's on you.

Where do you think you're going?

Why don't you get going, little fella,
before you hurt yourself?

Plankton?

It's Plank-Ton!

Come on down from there, little fella.

You wouldn't want to get hurt.

Come out, come out, wherever you are!

My eye!

He's getting away!

Ready for a Plank-Ton of bubbles?

The formula, please.

Come on. Team up with me.
We'll be rich and powerful!

No, thanks.

I'm already part of a teamwork.

Can we do hands in the middle again?

Yes, we can, Patrick.

But this time, there's one more
hand to go in the middle.

Plankton?

Oh, no.

Here you go, Krabs.

She's all yours.

This doesn't have
another insulting note in it, does it?

No, that's the old me.

The one who turned his back
on everything important

just to have that formula
all to himself.

But I realize now that keeping
something to myself is...

Selfish.

Especially when that something
is the Krabby Patty.

Okay, everybody, let's get back
to Bikini Bottom and...

Oh, no! I don't have the page!

Oh, no!

It must be back on Pelican Island!

Don't worry. I thought of everything.

All right, SpongeBob, take us home.

Thanks.

- Squidward!
- Oh, yeah.

Come on, it's time to go back
and open up The Krusty Krab!

Are you out of your patty-flipping mind?

I'll never leave this place!

I mean, look at me. I'm a god!

No, Squidward, you're a cashier.

Wait a minute! What? No!

Well, it was fun while it lasted.

Don't be sad, Squidward.

I left you a little surprise
under your shirt!

Rock-hard abs!

Aw, SpongeBob, you're okay in my book.

Aw, shucks.

Excuse us! We'd like
3,000 Krabby Patties, please!

That sound must mean
things are back to normal.

Who wants 3,000 Krabby Patties?

First one's for you, Gary.

Extra mayo, just the way you like it.

Caught you red-handed!

Gary hates mayo.

Plankton!
Up to your old tricks again already, eh?

Hey, I'm just putting things
back the way they were.

What do you have
to say about this, Gary?

Oh, shrimp.

See you later, tee-am-mate!

- Now can we sing it?
- Yeah!

Pwease, Mr. Piwate?

Oh, Kyle...

How can I say no to you?

Are you ready, kids?

- Aye-aye, Captain!
- Aye-aye, Captain!

What did you say?

There's sand in my ears
and I can't hear you!

- Aye-aye, Captain!
- Aye-aye, Captain!

Who lives in a pineapple under the sea?

SpongeBob SquarePants!

Absorbent and yellow and porous is he!

SpongeBob SquarePants!

If nautical nonsense
be something you wish #

SpongeBob SquarePants!

Then drop on the deck
and flop like a fish! #

- # SpongeBob SquarePants! #
- Ready?

SpongeBob SquarePants!

SpongeBob SquarePants!

Silence!

Oh, man. I like that song.
What happened?

I don't like that song
and I put an end to it.

Well, this music is terrible.

I suppose you're entitled to your...

Wait. Why am I talking to you?

You're an inferior species

What could you know about taste?

You get excited by
a pile of trash on a plate #

While I'm a spacetime traveler
Fabric unraveler #

Saving the Patty's in the past
But now I'm rapping ya #

That song's so bad
That I can't even stand it #

Dispense with this nonsense at once

I demand it!

You all stand no chance

Against my power
Don't try it #

Just sit there
with your flappy beak shut #

And be quiet!

Hold up, fish guts

- # You can't insult us #
- # The Seagull crew #

We're in no mood to hear... from you!

We're floating on the breeze
Party in seven seas #

You got your nose on your head

You blow up when you sneeze

Why's this guy so mean?

'Cause he's older than a fossil

All alone up in space

Yeah, that must be awful

Here, knock it off!
Yer making the movie too long! #

Why don't you take us back in time

So we can finish our song?

Fine.

SpongeBob SquarePants!

That was pretty good, actually.

Yeah, sorry!

This dance is so last year.

You know what this needs?

A little interpretive dance!

Made in the USA
Las Vegas, NV
10 March 2024

87007925R00046